Lorraine S. Kimball

Bustling For The Wedding Gown

A Guide for The Bride and Her Seamstress

ISBN: 1-4392-6213-6
ISBN-13: 9781439262139

To order additional copies, please contact us.
BookSurge
www.booksurge.com
1-866-308-6235
orders@booksurge.com

DEDICATION

This little book is dedicated to the memory of Mother, Father and Grandmother and to my Brother, Ken, for his understanding and belief that "It's All Good!"

TABLE OF CONTENTS

ACKNOWLEDGEMENTS

I've tried within the pages of this guide to help make everyone's wedding day more beautiful. I hope the ideas and techniques presented will benefit the bride and add to making her wedding day spectacular!

I also greatly thank my friends as well as my colleagues in this crazy wedding business. Their sound advice over the years is much appreciated.

And, of course, many many thanks to all my clients for their ideas and suggestions which helped me learn and grow and for trusting me to do a good job on their wedding gown.

Introduction

What is Bustling?

When I talk to a client about what alterations she needs for her wedding gown, often the answer goes something like this: "Well, I know I need a hem and it doesn't fit on top and it's too big (or too small) in the waist and, oh, the Sales Lady told me I need it bustled. Can you tell me what that is?"

Why is Bustling Important?

Bustling is needed when the wedding gown (or any special occasion dress for that matter) has a train that is part of the dress. What that means is the back skirt part is longer than the front and can extend out a few inches or many feet. In order for the wearer of the dress to easily move around the extra length has to be pulled over (over bustle) or tucked up (under bustle) so that the length of the skirt is uniform from front to back. This book explains some style as well as practical considerations to accomplish this.

Brides often ask me, "Why doesn't the dress already come bustled?" Some manufacturers are starting to add some bustles to dresses; however, they probably are reluctant to completely add the bustles because the exact height and shape of the bride will affect how the bustle will look. The under bustle technique, however, discussed in this book can safely be used by the manufacturer since the bustles are adjustable.

And, of course, if you want to avoid the process altogether you can choose a wedding gown with a detachable train. This type of train attaches to the back of the dress usually with hooks and eyes and is removable! These types of trains (and their pitfalls) will be discussed at the end of this book in Chapter VI.

ॐ∽

When is the Bustling Done?

Bustling is done after the ceremony and usually after the photographer takes some pictures with the train spread out. There is a ribbon loop usually sewn by manufacturers on the inside of the dress (center seam near the end of the train) which you can slip around your wrist and this allows you to pick up the train and keep it off the ground as you walk around and get in and out of the car or limousine.

Oh yes, and it is important to pick a CALM, not-easily-rattled person to bustle your dress. A team of two is also good! Since this is done right after the ceremony and before the reception (and usually after you get out of the car or limousine and have arrived at the reception site), it has to be done quickly. Don't pick any Bustler who caves under pressure! Sometimes your four-year old Ring Bearer is the best choice!

ॐ∽

Different Styles of Bustling

Now that we know that the objective of bustling is to get the extra train material off the floor, there are two techniques (as well as combinations) to accomplish this:

1)   Over bustle
2)   Under bustle

In either technique specific "points" are selected on the skirt and these points are used to gather the material to raise the hem off the floor. The next page displays two diagrams showing how the over bustle and the under bustle are done.

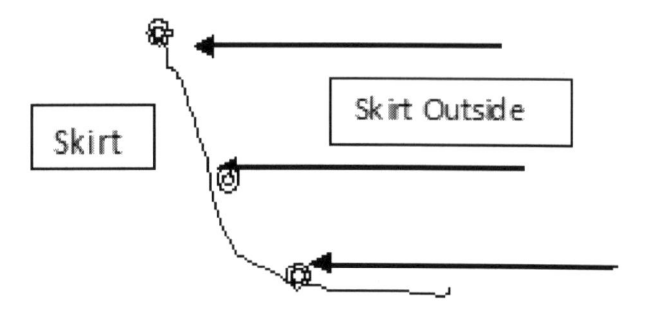

Figure 1. Over Bustle

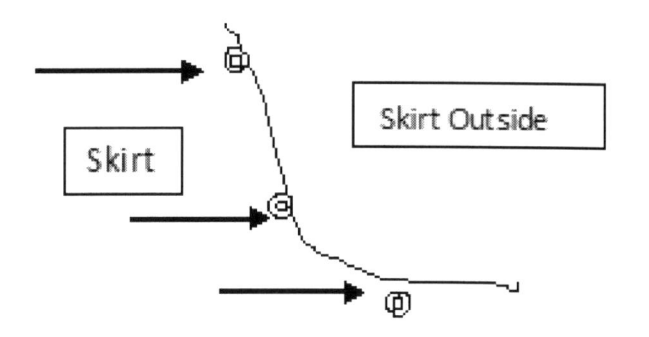

Figure 2. Under Bustle

Various factors influence what kind of bustling should be selected. Since the train is down during the ceremony it is of primary importance how the bride looks from the back since most of the guests view the wedding ceremony seeing the backs of the bride and groom. The bustling "points" should not be easily seen and should not "bunch up" the lining and the dress. Generally speaking, once the dress is bustled all the brides have the following design goals uppermost in their minds:

1) The dress or skirt (if a two-piece wedding gown) has to be off the floor so that the bride can walk and safely navigate the dance floor.

2) The bustling design should not make the bride's hips and/or derrier look like a "freight train".

3) The bustling should "hold " through the reception or the Hora dance. The Hora dance is done at the Jewish ceremony when the bride and groom (sitting on chairs) are passed above the reception guests. This can be very worrisome if the dress is not well bustled.

4) The bustling technique should be simple enough so that someone can easily bustle the gown for the bride. Although a lot of stores bustle the gowns using hooks and eyes, that technique is NOT used in this book since it has been my experience that these do not hold (i.e., once the bride sits down the hooks are lifted off the eyes, and the bustling comes undone).

❧ ❧

Tools and Skills You Will Need to Do Bustling

Here are the tools you will need to accomplish the bustling:

1. Needle
2. Thread or bustling thread (Yes, this is available through specialty stores)

3. Satin Ribbon (under bustle or combination bustle)
4. Buttons (if you are not going to use what is on the dress)

You also need to know a little about sewing (i.e., how to thread a needle and do a thread chain), but other than that the bustling process requires very little sewing. One thing about practice—you can get really good at this over time!

Here are some tips to make sure you have no dress disasters:

1. Make sure that while you are sewing the bustle (or doing it for the bride) you have no vibrant-colored nail polish on your nails which might transfer to the dress material—some of these nail polishes can smear.
2. Make sure your hands are smooth. Rough edges on your hands might put a run in the fabric.
3. Do NOT wear any jewelry which could damage the dress because it accidentally catches and puts a run in the tulle, organza, or satin.
4. Work with plenty of light and when you are not tired. Really good seamstresses can get just plain tired and then the bustling (which is done last) doesn't turn out as beautiful as it can be.

And for Heaven's Sake, have fun!

Chapter I
Determining the Bustling Design

There are several major factors which should be considered when creating a perfect bustling pattern scheme:

1) The bride's height and shape
2) The shape of the train
3) The fabric drapability
4) The decoration on the train and back of the dress
5) The look from the front of the dress (i.e., avoid the "wings")

These factors all work together in determining which approach to use. This is much more of an art than a science, and sometimes those logical it-should-be-done-this-way sewing skills need to be bent a little to create the right look. It is important to leave enough time to do it properly! The bustling is just as important as any other alteration to the dress.

The Bride's Height and Shape

The petite bride has, of course, a shorter distance from her waist to the floor and therefore more of the train will be on the floor, and more fabric will need to be bustled. This is an extra challenge because of the inverse relationship (i.e., more fabric, less space to pull it up!). The over bustle/under bustle combination discussed later in the technique section works well for the petite bride since the look elongates the silhouette.

The taller bride can often have fewer bustle points since the amount of fabric on the floor and the distance from her waist to the floor are more manageable. The tiers on an under bustle can be two or three where on a petite bride sometimes four or five tiers are needed.

Whether the bride is thin or not-so-thin, the objective is to keep the folds of material aesthetically pleasing. No bride likes to accentuate the hip area!

ॐॐ

The Shape of the Train

The more fabric in the train, the more points are required to properly "take up" the gown. The very full sweep train will have many bustle points (especially on a petite bride) in order for all the fabric to be pulled off the floor. The thinner train, or the less full skirt with the long train can often be a "bustling nightmare". Bustle points need to be engineered with smaller tucks since the skirt around the hip area does not have as much fabric.

ॐॐ

The fabric drapability

The "hand" of the fabric is rather an old term that refers to the drapability of the fabric. If a person picks up the corner of the fabric, either the fabric will fall in soft folds, or it won't! A stiff fabric will drape differently than a softer fabric in a bustling pattern. This will affect the choice of bustling options; i.e., certain fabrics such as organza, will often need smaller tucks so that the bustling has a pretty result.

The Decoration on the Train and Back of the Dress

In choosing what type of bustling option to select, careful attention should be given to the beading or embroidery pattern on the back of the dress or skirt. One of the major goals of bustling is to display this pattern beautifully since this is a major factor in the cost of the dress.

The Look From the Front of the Dress

The bustling when completed should not affect the front silhouette of the dress. That is, if it is an A-line dress, it should still look like an A-line dress without bunches of fabric showing in the back. If it is a full-cut skirt, it should still be a full-cut skirt with enough points or tucks so that the silhouette is still basically the same. It is the goal always to have the side seams of the dress not to be "pulled back" in the bustle, or drag on the floor. Sometimes, though, this is nearly impossible on some dresses and sometimes it is necessary to break (or at least bend) these rules—do whatever works!

Chapter II
How to do the Over Bustle

The over bustle as we learned in the Introduction section has the fabric pulled up and over to the waist. It is used a lot in bustling the dress with a tulle skirt since that is easy to bustle and since the dress is very poufy anyway, it is not a style disconnect. Before you start, you will need to measure how much the train is on the floor.

Make sure the bride is wearing the shoes she is going to wear at the wedding and reception since the heel height is very important—i.e., you need to make sure that the fabric is OFF the ground! It is especially easy to slip on tulle, so you want to make sure that especially with this fabric it is not dragging on the ground.

Measuring For the Amount to Bustle

Have the bride try on her dress with the shoes she will be wearing. If she is going to change into lower heels for the reception, use those. Spread the train out on the floor and measure the amount to be bustled:

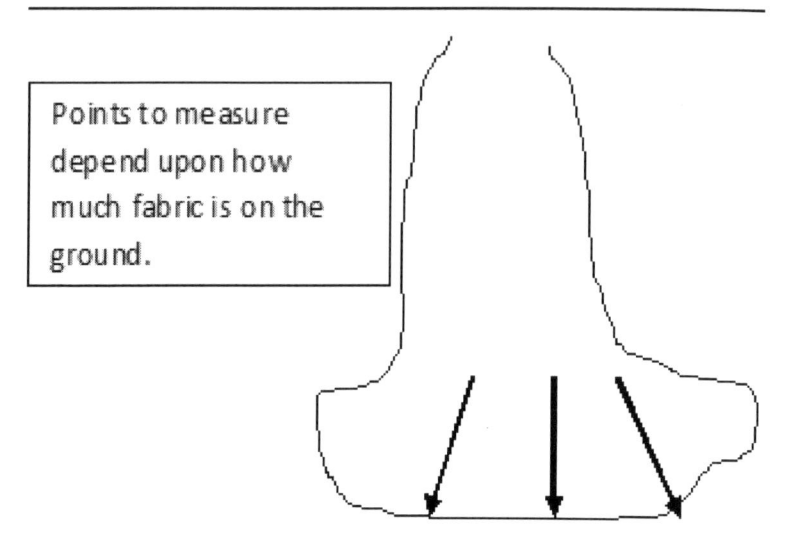

Points to measure depend upon how much fabric is on the ground.

Figure 3. Over Bustle measurements for Points

Now observe the waistline of the dress. Are there buttons available so that you can pick up the dress, sew a loop and fasten the loops to the existing buttons? If not, you will have to pick points along the waistline where you can sew buttons which "blend in" to the design of the dress, or are hidden by a pleat. For instance, on a dress with some crystal accents, I choose a clear crystal button to attach to the waistline. With pearls, you can use pretty pearl buttons.

You can also make your own bustling ornament, in which case you will be sewing loops at the waist and at the bustling point on the dress and hooking both together with the ornament (see "Making a Two Loop Over Bustle"—pg 15).

If you are going to "hide" the buttons in a pleat at the waist, then pick a flat button that will not show very much, as in the following diagram:

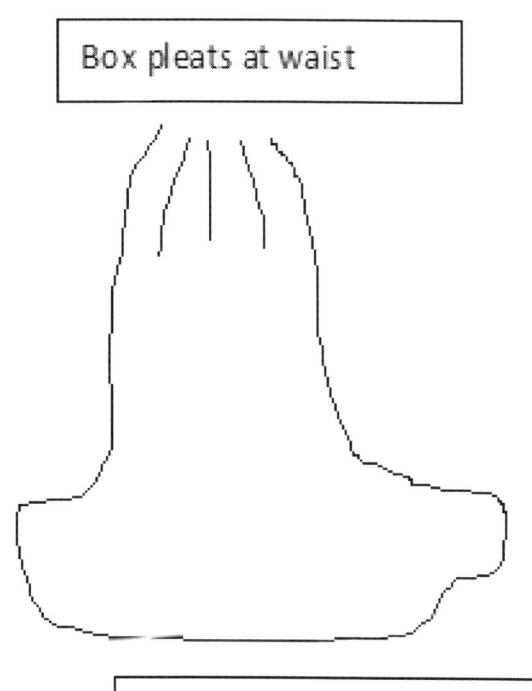

Box pleats at waist

Sew either one button under one pleat or a button under EACH pleat.

Figure 4. Sewing Positions for Box Pleat Over Bustle

You can either sew one button under one pleat (and only do one loop on the dress) or sew a button under each pleat and do two loops on the dress. I usually do two loops because then the bustling loops are redundant (i.e., if one breaks due to a size 13 man's shoe stepping on the train) then the other one will hold. Also, on the two bustling loops you can make it into a butterfly to disguise the fact that there are bustling loops—this is REALLY a butterfly that has landed on the dress for good luck!

Now that the basic measuring has been done, start planning the bustle. I use safety pins to pin the bustle to the waistline so that I can check the bustling design and make sure that the bustling is pretty.

Start with the center seam and pin through all fabric layers at the point where you are going to sew the button. For example, if the train is 15 inches on the floor, then you will need to do a bustling point 15 inches down from the waist at the back seam (i.e., you need to "take up" 15 inches):

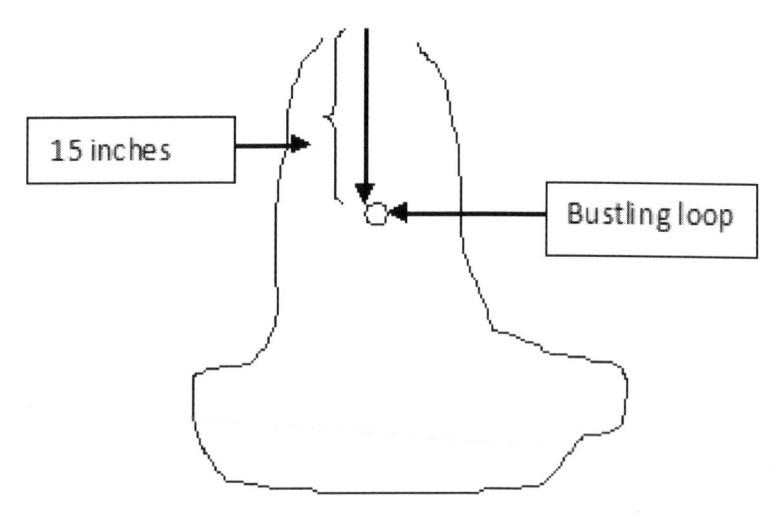

Figure 5. Planning the Points on An Over bustle

Make sure all the center seams of each layer of fabric are lined up. Sometimes it is easier to take the dress and lay it flat on a cutting board and then pin it. Attach a safety pin to the waist where the skirt is going to be attached. Emulate how the finished bustle will look by taking the bustle point safety pin and attaching it to the other safety pin at the waist. Do the same thing with the other bustle points that you have measured. If you have measured three points you will have three safety pins at the waist and three safety pins on the skirt. Try to select places on the skirt which have seams or applique. These points provide more stability for the bustle points and more opportunity to hide the loops, if desired. Make some fabric swatch squares (1" x 1" or 2" by 2"). This fabric square is placed on the very under side of the skirt. Pin the planned points through to the fabric swatches, which provide extra stability. When you are all done on a very full skirt, you could have five or seven points on the skirt where you have pinned the bustling points.

The next step is to check the design to make sure that the fabric backing squares are not visible from the outside of the dress and there are no lumps, bumps, and bulges. Lumps, bumps, and bulges are to be avoided! This is a visual inspection to see how the planned bustles look with the bride standing in the dress. If a lot of fabric is being picked up then you could have lumpy bustles at the hipline, which is not a good thing! If the fabric drapes well, then the folds created will be close to the body and will be quite beautiful.

On tulle or organza over satin, and some satins, the fabric and the lining, interfacing, and fabric (remember, all of them have to be worked as one) will create too much of a bulge. You can either scrap the plan to do an over bustle and choose an under bustle instead, or you can minimize the amount of fabric in the bustle by doing smaller bustles or a combination of over bustles and under bustles.

If you try to minimize the amount of fabric bunching at the waist, it is oftentimes helpful to make the center bustle two points rather than one, as in the following diagram:

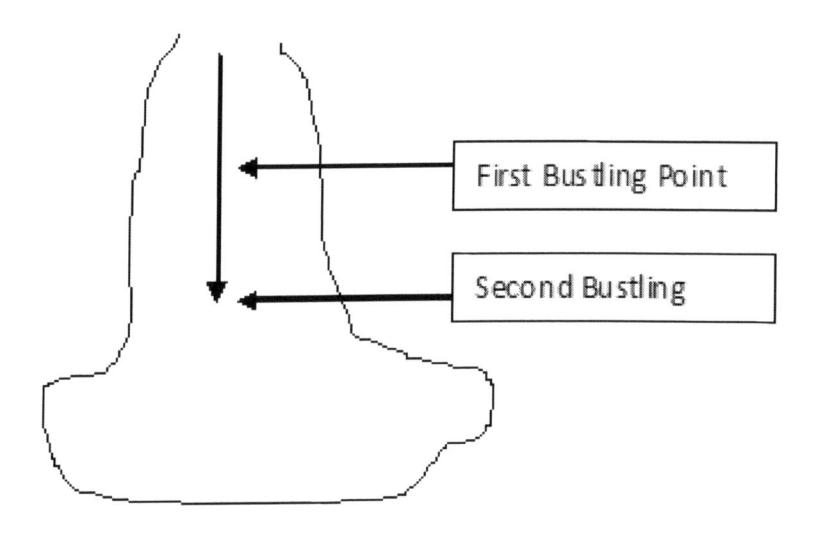

Figure 6. Diagram of Bustling Points to Minimize Fabric at Waist

By doing two bustling points the fabric will be forced to lay flatter. It does, however, depend on the cut of the train and how much fabric the bride needs in the high hip area. This looks good in a number of cases—you need to try it and see what it looks like. I call this the "waterfall" bustle and it is discussed again at the end of this chapter.

⊱⊰

Threading The Needle and Chain Loop(s)

Now, we are ready to start! Choose a sharp needle so you will not risk putting a run in the fabric. You want to be careful NOT to stick yourself, of course, because it is a no-no to bleed on the dress! Sometimes I will wear those thin plastic gloves—not the kind that you get to scour the sink, but the ones that come 50 or 100 to the pack and are thin. It takes some practice working with these, but at least you are sure the dress remains clean. This section covers chaining your own thread; however, if you want to use bustling thread (or a chain from your serger) that's okay also.

Thread the needle with a good thread (the same color as the fabric) so that there are two or four threads:

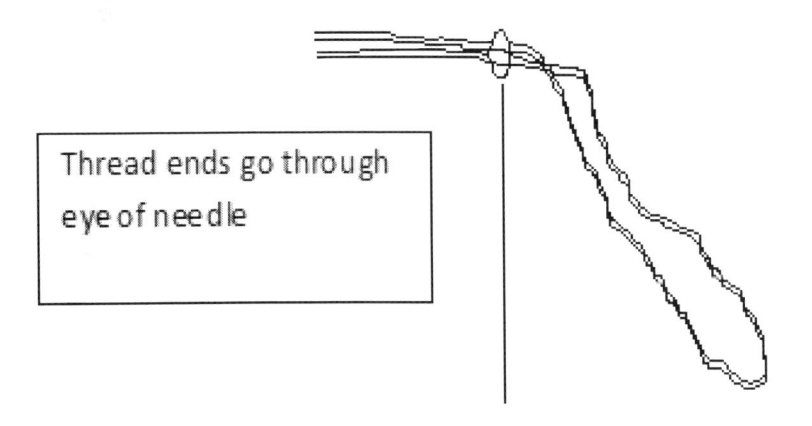

Thread ends go through
eye of needle

Figure 7. Diagram of Threading Needle for Over-Bustle

Starting on the outside of the dress, insert the needle from the outside at the bustle point, through the fabric and backing, back to the outside and through the loop. This eliminates the need to tie a knot (which may pull out). The following illustration shows this step:

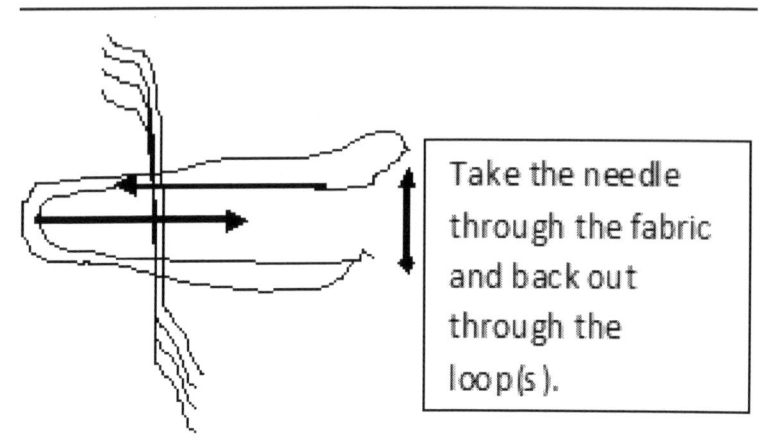

Take the needle through the fabric and back out through the loop(s).

Figure 8. Starting The Loop

Take one more pass through the fabric, leaving a loop on the outside in order to do the chain loop. Hold the loop in your left hand (or right hand if you are left-handed), and make a chain, much like crocheting:

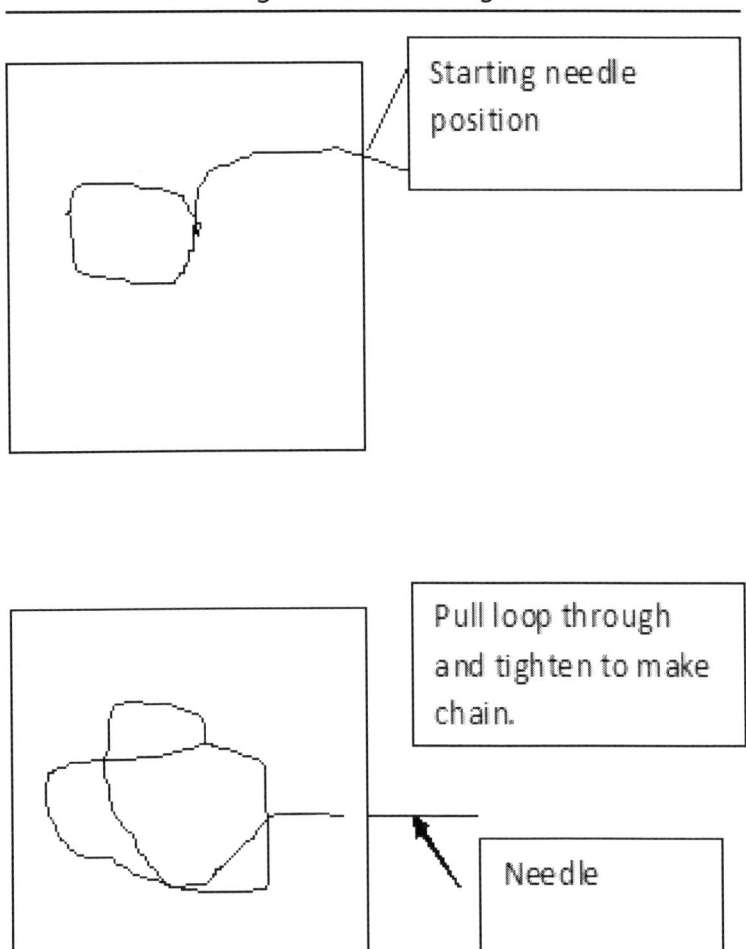

Starting needle position

Pull loop through and tighten to make chain.

Needle

Figure 9. Starting The Chain On The Loop

Continue this chaining (pull loop through and tight) until you have the desired length to go around the bustling button. Keep the loops tight and finish off by putting the needle through the fabric and back out through the ending chain loop. This will secure the loops. On the underside tie a knot, take one more stitch through the backing, and tie another knot. This will ensure that the loop does not pull through. Test the bustle loop by hanging it on the button. The finished loop will look something like this (enlarged view):

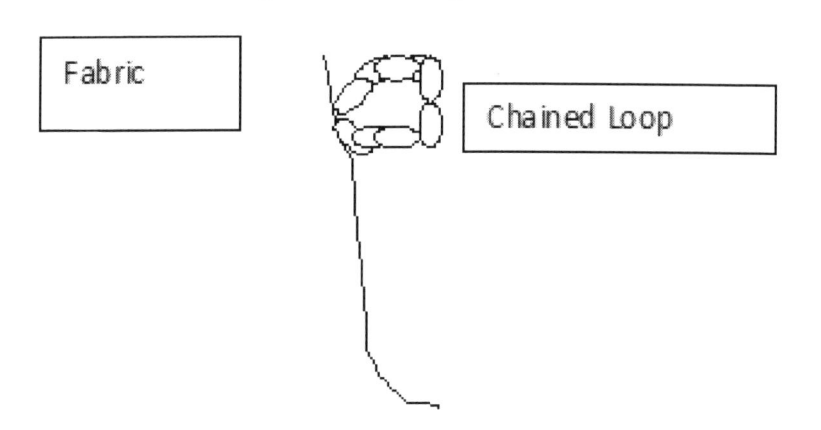

Figure 10. Finished Chain

If you would like to do another loop, start the threading of the needle all over again and make the second loop very close to the first one. You can make it into a butterfly by decorating the center with beads:

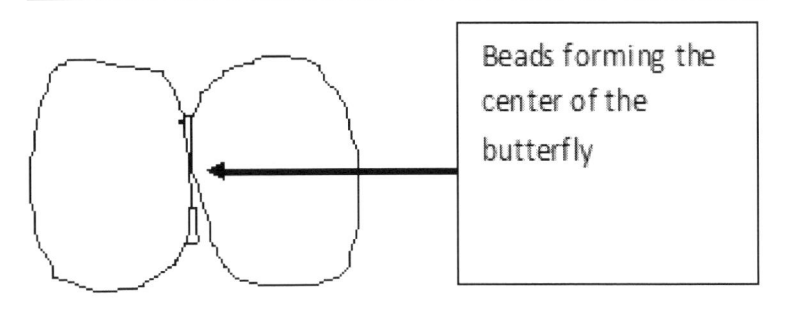

Beads forming the center of the butterfly

Figure 11. Example Of The Butterfly Loop

Tired yet? We have only begun to bustle!!

🙠 🙢

Sewing the Buttons To The Waist Area.

If you are using the existing buttons on the dress to hang the loops, make sure the buttons are secure. A lot of manufacturers try to save time by sewing on the center back buttons with one continuous thread, so that when you try to use the button to hang fabric, the thread either pops or pulls out all the buttons! Not good.

Sewing on the buttons is easy, right? Well, sometimes yes, sometimes no. If the dress is constructed with heavy interfacing I will sometimes use a very thin, sharp beading needle to sew on the button. You want to make sure that the button is securely sewn to the dress because it will be used to support the weight of the fabric. If you are sewing on the underside of a pleat, it is useful to have the dress on a flat surface.

Making a Two-Loop Over Bustle.

Well, sometimes you don't want to use buttons if they "stand out" and interfere with the design of the dress. For instance, in slinky gowns it is sometimes better to use the following method:

Where you would normally sew the buttons, sew another chained loop instead. If you are using a pin to attach both loops the loops need not be as large as to loop around a button. Then, you can either use a pin or make a pin with a button on the underside and use this to put the loops together, as follows:

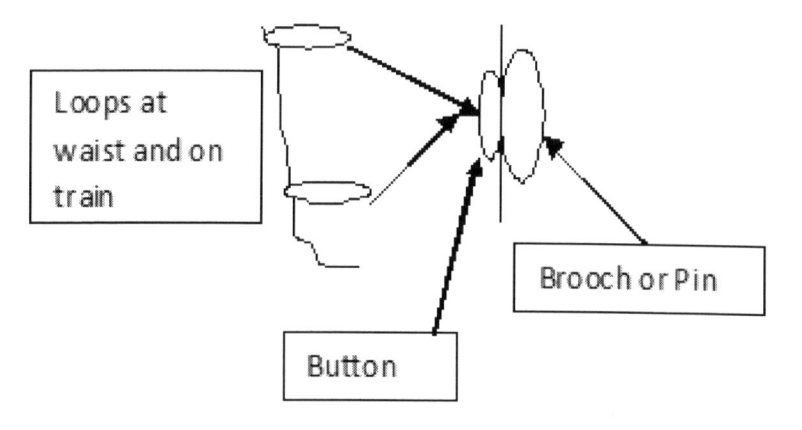

Figure 12. Diagram of Loops Attached With Pin

❧∾❧

Two Point (Waterfall Bustle)

Before leaving this over bustle section another technique deserves some mention because it is useful in some dresses so that there are no "wings" seen from the front of the dress.

Every bride is worried about "wings"—either those fluffy love handles which seem to pop out over that strapless dress, or the "wings" created by not properly bustling

the dress. In this instance, the fabric will make unflattering pleats because too deep a pleat is made with draping the fabric. The solution to this is to first do the center bustle to pick up the fabric off the floor. Then, pick a place between the first bustle point and the button to sew another loop. Both loops go over the same button.

The following pages contain a few pictures of dresses where the over bustle technique has been used.

Picture 1. Over Bustle On Full Skirt Using Buttons.

Picture 2. Over Bustle Using One Point

Picture 3. Two Point (Waterfall Over Bustle)

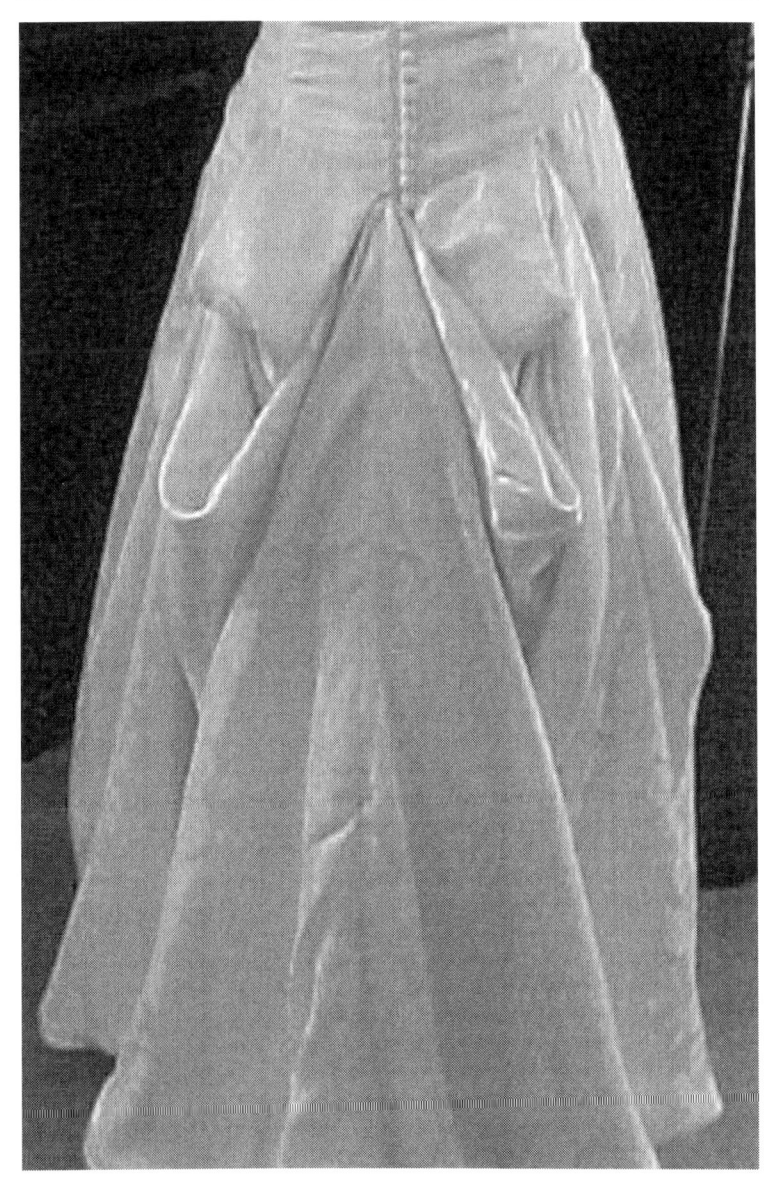

Picture 4. The Box Pleat Over Bustle

Picture 5. The Over Bustle Using Loops and Pin

Chapter III
How to do the Under Bustle

The under bustle is also known as the Austrian or French bustle and differs from the over bustle since the skirt is "tucked up" and fastened under the skirt. I have seen some creative ways of accomplishing this! One dress I re-bustled had curtain rings under the skirt! On other dresses, you will find ribbons hanging from the inside of the dress, which are numbered so you know which ones to tie together. This kind of reminds me of the Lewis & Clark Caverns a lot!

I have developed my own technique which is described in this chapter. I have tried different things over the years to see what works best, and I have now come up with something that is relatively easy to do for creating beautiful bustles.

Measuring For the Amount to Bustle

You want to start this process the same as you did for the over bustle technique. Have the bride try on her dress with the shoes she will be wearing and measure the amount on the floor:

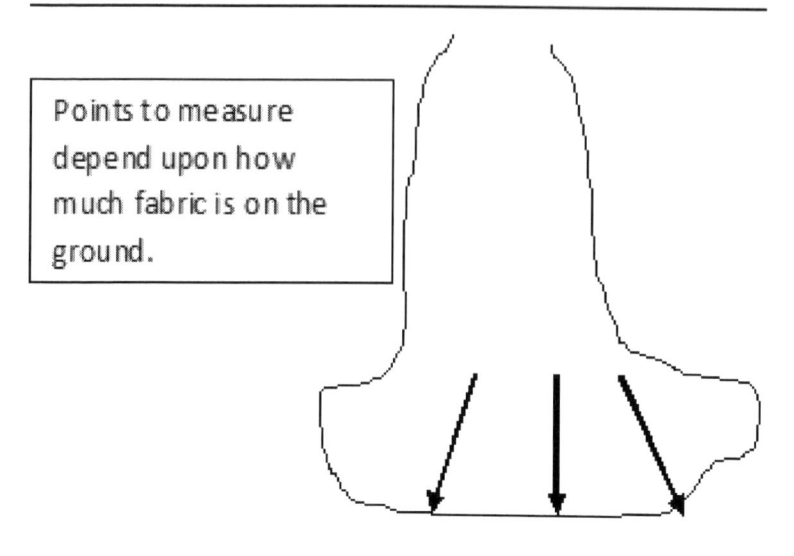

Points to measure depend upon how much fabric is on the ground.

Figure 13. Measure Length To Be Bustled.

The under bustle involves taking tucks (or horizontal pleats) in the fabric and fastening the material at points under the skirt. If the bride is petite, the amount of material you want to tuck should be less. This is also true of a fabric that does not drape easily; i.e., such as a silk fabric. Generally, I try to keep the pleating to no more than 12-15 inches, which give you a tuck in the fabric of about 6 – 7 1/2 inches (half that amount). When you are bustling organza over satin, you may have to make even smaller pleats since the organza tends to be very stiff and will create volume on the outside of the skirt.

Sometimes the train has a panel decoration or is made up of two separate pieces and each will have to be bustled separately. Those situations will be covered toward the end of this chapter.

The Mother Fish and the Baby Fish

I came up with this terminology as a way of explaining how to do the bustles to mothers of the bride and attendants. To create the bustle you will need several yards of ribbon. This varies with the amount of bustles you need, and I usually purchase about five yards to make sure I have enough. Select a good satin ribbon in white, ivory, or pastels (if you want to color code your work). I like the 5/8 inch width to work with. If you are using ivory or pastels, MAKE SURE that the ribbons don't show to the outside of the dress. There are some dresses with chiffon overlays that I have selected 1/8" ribbon ties so that they are not visible.

Now, make several loops with the ribbon (i.e., these are the mother fishes). This is going to be the start of the bustle and will be sewn to the lining or sewn-in petticoat of the dress. When I have time I sew these loops on the sewing machine, but that is not necessary—you can also sew them by hand. Take a length of ribbon 6 ½ ", and fold in half. Keeping the cut edges together, fold the ribbon twice, creating a loop. Stitch the folded part of the ribbon (either by machine or hand) to create the loop. The finished product should look like this:

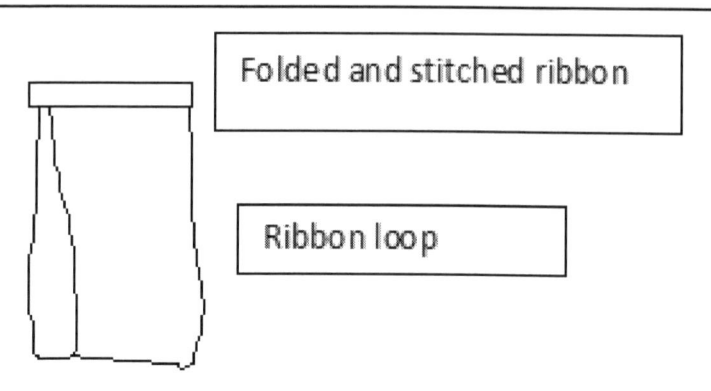

Folded and stitched ribbon

Ribbon loop

Figure 14. Diagram Showing Starting Loops

Make five of these. You may not need all of them, depending upon the results desired.

Start sewing these on the lining or the sewn-in petticoat of the dress. If the dress lining and outer fabric are sewn together, you want to sew these loops to the petticoat. If the lining is separate, sew these loops to the lining. Sew the first ribbon loop on the center seam as high on the hip line as you can (i.e., usually just below the zipper). You want to make sure that you do not sew this loop to the dress, because if you do you will create a "ski-slope" effect on the outside of the dress, like this:

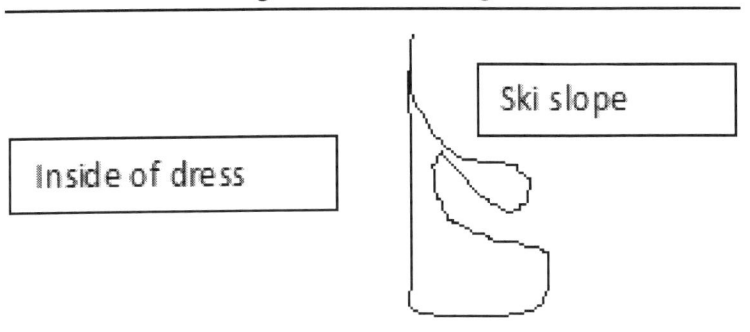

Figure 15. Illustration Of The Ski Slope Effect

This is only a good thing if the bride happens to be marrying her ski instructor!

You are now going to go down the center seam and create a series of "baby fish" loops to tie into the mother loop creating a series of tucks in the center back of the gown.

So how many tucks should you take? Take the original measurement (i.e., the amout of fabric on the floor) and divide by 15 inches (the tuck). In most dresses the resulting number will be 3 or 4 tucks. The tucks do not have to be uniform. For instance, you can make the starting tuck smaller than the tucks toward the end of the train. It is better to go from a smaller tuck near the waist to larger tucks nearer the floor.

These "baby" loops are created by taking about a 24 – 28 inch piece of ribbon, folding it in half and stitching the last 1 ½—2 inches, creating both a tie and a loop on the same piece of ribbon. The finished product will look like this:

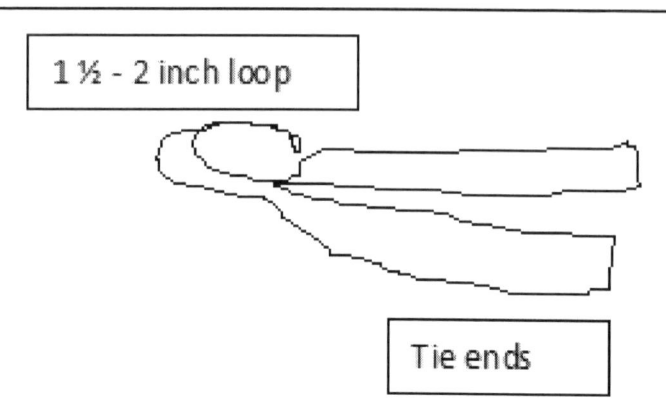

Figure 16. Construction Of The Loop/Tie Combinations

Sew the first loop/tie combination the number of inches down which you have measured for your first tuck. You can use your hand to tuck up the material to the sewn loop to visualize the pleat occurring on the outside of the dress before sewing on the tie/loop combination. When you have picked a point to sew this loop/tie combination, sew the "baby fish" with the ties pointing upward toward the waist, at the place where you have previously created the loop. This resulting tie/loop combination will then be tied into the first loop creating the pleat on the outside of the dress. Take one of the ties, thread it through the "mother loop", and tie a bow with the two ends. The following picture illustrates how the dress will look with the first loop tied:

Picture 6. The Start of the Under Bustle

It is important to now note that these ties are adjustable. Although I start by making the bow tight, since the ties are long you can leave some space. If after you are all done the dress is too high off the floor—just leave a couple of inches slack when tying the ribbons which will allow the tucks to be lower.

When you look at the above picture you will notice that there is still material on the floor. Usually the whole bustling process cannot be done with just one bustle in the center (i.e., only if the train is relatively short can you accomplish this).

Continue the process by going down the center seam and pick another point to tie the second "baby fish" loop. This second set of ties will tie into the first "baby loop" that you created. Usually you will want the pleats on the outside of the skirt to have a cascading effect. The following picture illustrates this concept:

Picture 7. Two Center Loops Tied

Continue down the center seam until all the material at the center is off the ground. Usually this will require 2-3 tiers. When you are done the following picture illustrates what the dress will look like from the outside:

Picture 8. Center Bustling Completed

You will notice that you still may not be finished because the left and right-hand side of the train may still be on the floor.

Now, you start the process over by sewing a main "mother" loop at the left high hip area—again, on the lining or sewn-in petticoat. This loop should be sewn a little lower than the center loop because, of course, the left and right sides of the train are not as long as the center of the train. I usually make it about 5-6 inches lower. This also has a more pleasing look on the outside of the dress since the folds are at different places.

Sew a loop on the same level at the right side. Both the left and right side loops should be toward the back, rather than the front, of the dress. On a very full skirt you will need maybe as many as five or seven starting loops and you don't have to worry about sewing the loops too forward since the dress is full anyway; i.e., you will not be interfering with the dress design.

After the loops are sewn, find points on the gown to sew the loop/tie combinations. Remember, this is an art rather than a science. I try to select a point on the gown where there is already a seam or an applique. Then, when I do the sewing, the threads showing on the outside of the dress are hidden. Yes, because you need to sew the loops through the lining to the outside of the dress and back, you will see some stitches. I try to make them as tiny as possible or hide them in a seam. If you have a beaded dress it is sometimes pretty to sew a pearl or bead on the point where you have sewn the bustling point—do whatever looks best.

The final product looks like the picture on the following page.

Picture 9. Final Under-Bustled Gown

One more comment before we close the under-bustle chapter. Sometimes a dress calls for you to start from the bottom up (i.e., especially those dresses with a panel decoration on the back of the train). In this case the loops and ties at the bottom of the dress are done first. They will line up on the bottom third of the petticoat. Then the other bustles are tucked by seeing how much additional fabric has to be pulled up. The bustle design is done so that the panel is displayed. This allows for a more structured look, which is more pleasing to some clients.

Chapter IV
How to do the Over/Under Bustle Combination

Sometimes the best look is accomplished by a combination of the over bustle and under bustle.

This technique is especially useful when the train has some pretty pattern in a triangle. The first point is selected at the top, or beginning of the pattern and the first loop for the over-bustle technique is created at the top of the pattern. When the dress is over bustled to the waist, the pattern is displayed beautifully. Sometimes to keep the outer part of the dress in the correct shape, I will sew tiny loops on either side of the pattern, which loops over a bead on the dress. Generally, though, you don't need to do anything and the pattern remains displayed because the fabric is very thick with all the beading.

A word about heavily-beaded dresses—they will be quite heavy when they are bustled. You have to be aware of this on the dance floor since you will not be used to moving around in such a heavy dress.

If the over bustle does NOT take the left and right side of the dress off the floor, I do an under bustle "tuck" technique on the left and right side of the dress. The starting loops are sewn lower on the lining or the petticoat since they are generally just taking up inches of fabric rather than a few feet.

And guess what? Sometimes you will need to pick up extra fabric which is to the right and the left of immediate center. Some trains are shaped such that the sweep around the center at the end of the train is so full some extra tucking is needed. So, here comes the "duck tail" technique. When you need to pick up additional fabric right around the center of the train you can pick up the fabric just to the left and right of the lowest center tuck. Since nothing else is going to be tied into these tucks, you can just sew a strip of ribbon at these places. The "duck" is formed by sewing the left and right ribbons to the last center loop on the train. You'll see why I call it the "duck".

The following picture shows the final version using the over bustle/under bustle technique.

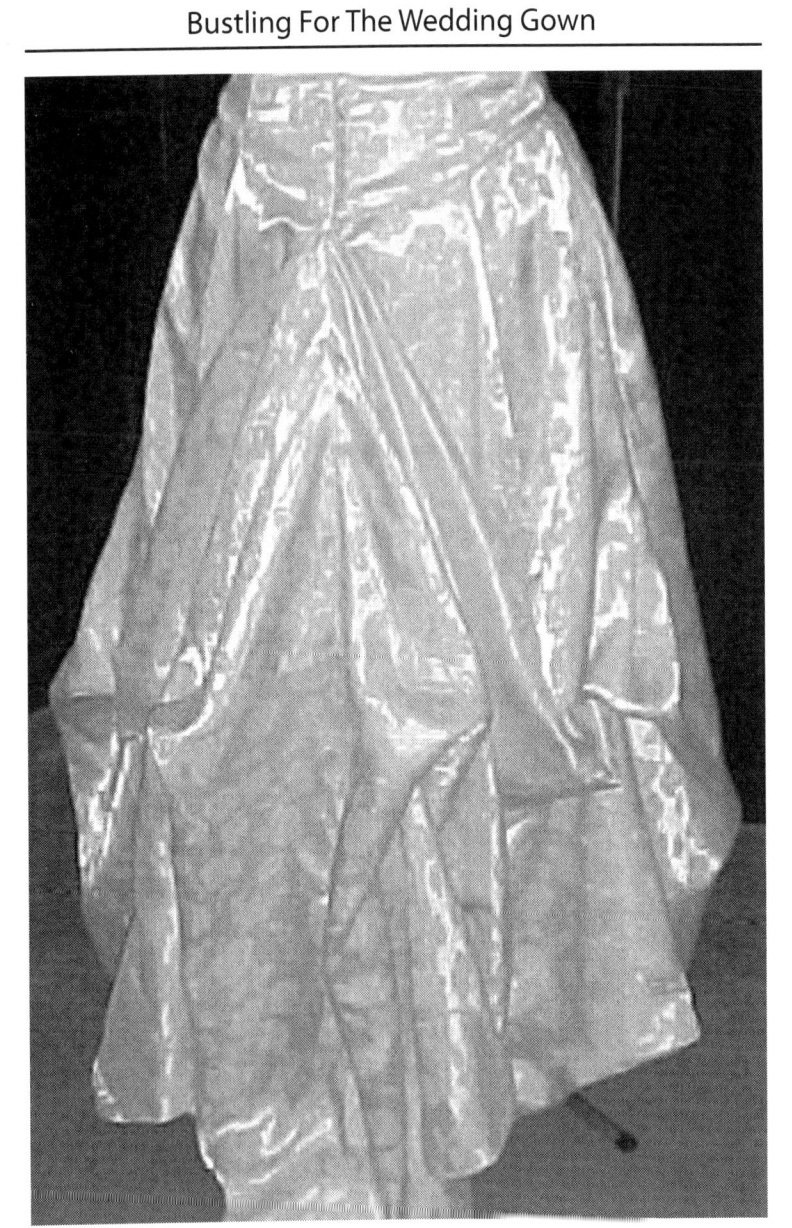

Picture 10. The Over Bustle/Under Bustle Technique

Chapter V
How to Do Unusual Bustles

Bustling the Already-Tucked Dress

There are some beautiful dresses out there that have tucks already, creating pretty tufted patterns all over the dress usually accented by beads. Again, you want to follow the design of these dresses.

What I usually do with these dresses is an under bustle technique to pull up the bottom layer under the skirt. The over bustle seems to create too much bulk—remember less is more. If you are altering the dress as well, you want to check the tufts already sewn into the dress since some might be loose already! Sometimes the crystal beads on the dress have acted like little saws and weakened the threads.

৵৹৵

Bustling the Multi-Layered Dress

And, of course, there is always that unusual layered dress which presents a great challenge. This includes drapey chiffon over satin, lace over satin, multi-layered satin dresses. Sometimes the best approach to bustling these dresses is to treat each layer separately.

I start with bustling the very inner layer first in order to see how the outer fabric looks. Most of the time I will end up under bustling the inner part of the dress and over bustling the outer portion. Chiffon as an outer layer can also look quite lovely under bustled. The challenge on chiffon is to make sure nothing shows to the outside of the dress.

Asymmetrical Gowns

And, of course, you will come across those asymmetrical gowns which look very pretty but are quite difficult to bustle. You may have to treat the left and right sides of the dress completely different and bustle each side separately. Make sure you estimate enough design time because it might take 1-4 tries to make it look right.

Chapter VI
Detachable Trains

If you have selected a gown with a detachable train, do a test to make sure it won't come undone even for the brief time you are going to have it attached. I suggest clients hook the train to the places either sewn on the dress or where eyes are sewn on the dress. Usually I replace thread eyes (which are very fragile and will not support the weight of the train) with metal ones. You also want to make sure that the dress is not pulled one way or the other by the weight of the train.

Since these trains can be quite long and full it is better to have flower girls hold the ends of the train as you walk down the aisle. Otherwise, it looks like the bride is dragging a drapery down the aisle and it will be very heavy!

Chapter VII
Bride's Guide to Minimize or Avoid Wedding Day Disasters

Here is a checklist of additional hints in order to minimize disasters—

- Do a partial bustling of the back right and left side of the dress if necessary so that no one Accidentally steps on the dress while accompanying you going down the aisle.
- Bring safety pins and thread and needle to do repairs if necessary.
- Make sure that ribbons and ties are off the floor and will NOT interfere with walking.
- Realize this is a special occasion dress. Act like a Princess—pick up your dress going up and down stairs and go slowly because sometimes you cannot see your feet. Those models and actresses you see in the movies and television have practiced for hours so they can glide down the stairs with effortless ease.

- Plan your trips to the ladies room if you have one of those poufy gowns. You will need extra time...

And Remember—The last thing you put on before going down the aisle is a smile!

75498916R00038

Made in the USA
Middletown, DE
05 June 2018